MW01254836

Courageous Care

Courageous Care: Helping Others Even When You're Afraid
Copyright © 2023 Kari Bartkus
All rights reserved.

No part of this publication may be reproduced in a retrieval system, or transmitted in any form or by any means—electronic, mechanical, photocopying, recording, or otherwise—without the prior written permission of the publisher.

All Scripture quotations taken from the Holy Bible, New Living Translation, copyright © 1996, 2004, 2015 by Tyndale House Foundation. Used by permission of Tyndale House Publishers, Inc., Carol Stream, Illinois 60188. All rights reserved.

This manuscript has undergone viable editorial work and proofreading, yet human limitations may have resulted in minor grammatical or syntax-related errors remaining in the finished book. The understanding of the reader is requested in these cases. While precaution has been taken in the preparation of this book, the publisher and author assume no responsibility for errors or omissions, or for damages resulting from the use of the information contained herein.

This book is set in the typeface *Athelas* designed by Veronika Burian and Jose Scaglione.

Cover Image: London Adelaide Photography
Instagram: @londonadelaidephotography, @ashleydmckinney, @singletondaily

Author Image: D.B. Johns Photography
Instagram: @dbjohns.photography

Some of this material first appeared on the Journal Gently podcast (formerly Let's Encourage One Another) and in the Courageous Care Masterclass, offered by Kari Bartkus.

For more resources, visit https://lovedoesthat.org.

Paperback ISBN: 978-1-955546-45-4

A Publication of *Tall Pine Books*
119 E Center Street, Suite B4A | Warsaw, Indiana 46580
www.tallpinebooks.com

| 1 23 23 20 16 02 |

Published in the United States of America

Courageous Care

Helping Others Even When You're Afraid

Kari Bartkus

Contents

Introduction ....*xi*

Section One: Courageously Compassionate

1. Uncertain 5

2. Unavailable 11

3. Unfamiliar 19

4. Uncomfortable 27

5. Unwilling 33

6. Which Obstacle Is It for You? 41

Section Two: Authentically Taking Action

7. Characteristics 51

8. Skills and Training 57

9. Experiences 63

10. Personality 69

11. Your Divine Design 75

Section Three: Relying on God

12. Why We Need Discernment in Caring for Others.. 85

13. Hearing the Sacred Echo 91

14. Recognizing God's Voice 95

15. Practicing the Examen 101

16. Recognizing God's Invitation to Reach Out............ 105

Section Four: Ever Mindful of the Other Person

17. Expressed Needs.............................. 115

18. Love Languages 121

19. Personality and Preferences 127

20. Closeness of Relationship.................... 131

21. Knowing Your Friend 135

Conclusion: Don't Let Fear Stop You.................. 143

Appendix A: Write Your Story 155

Appendix B: Scripture Writing...................... 157

References.................................. 160

About the Author............................ 161

The

C.A.R.E.

Framework

C A R E

COURAGEOUSLY   AUTHENTICALLY   RELYING   EVER MINDFUL OF
COMPASSIONATE   TAKING ACTION   ON GOD   THE OTHER PERSON

Introduction

Let's consider a pretty familiar story in the Bible: The Parable of the Good Samaritan. Only this time, I want to rewrite the parable a little bit.

Imagine you are walking throughout your day, and you come across different people in your life who are hurting.

In the morning, you get a message from a friend who is struggling with depression. She texts you that she needs prayer, she is having a hard time, and she doesn't know how to move forward that day. Not sure what to tell her, you text back that you're praying and then move on to the next part of your day.

Around lunchtime, you get a call from a friend who wants to get together for coffee. She's struggling in her marriage and needs someone to talk to. Feeling the pressure, you tell her you'd love to talk, but you're too busy today. Maybe next week? And on you go.

In the afternoon, your daughter gets home from school and obviously has had a hard day. You love her so much that it hurts *you* to see her hurting. So, you dive right into trying to cheer her up with her favorites: dinner at her choice of restaurant, an offer to get ice cream, and a board game when you get back home. But in doing so, you ignore what's really bothering her from school that day.

You, my friend, have others around you who are hurting and need your care and support. And you are feeling overwhelmed.

You want to help them, but you don't know how. You want to be there for them, but you're tired from all the things you're already doing. You want to fix it for them, but you know you can't.

And so too many times, you end up fading away into the background and doing nothing at all.

Do you want to know what stopped *me* from reaching out?

I was too introverted.

I didn't know what to say or do.

I felt like I was intruding or getting in the way.

What you'll learn in this book are lessons I've picked up along the way of caring for those around me who are hurting. And it will completely transform the way you reach out to your friends and neighbors and love them—*really love them*—when they are struggling.

Because, friend, there *is* a healthy way to care for those in your life. A way where you can see someone who is hurting and lovingly reach out to them.

By the time we're done, you'll have learned how to:

- Overcome five obstacles that get in the way of reaching out to those in your life who are hurting.
- Identify how God has divinely designed you (yes, *you*!) to care for your hurting friends.
- Hone in on God's voice so you can sense His sacred nudges.
- Ensure your care is meaningful to your friend.

You already *care*, so let's learn how to do so in a healthy, God-honoring way using an acronym that's easy to remember: C.A.R.E.

C: Courageously Compassionate

A: Authentically Taking Action

R: Relying on God

E: Ever Mindful of the Other Person

The first section is the hardest. Go gently and take a break when you need to, but don't let it stop you from moving forward when you're ready. God is with you!

SECTION ONE

C

COURAGEOUSLY
COMPASSIONATE

few years ago, I discovered there was a mama in our town whose elementary-aged son had cancer. I didn't know her personally, yet my heart went out to her. Watching your child suffer has got to be one of *the* hardest things *ever*.

She often posted updates to a Facebook page, so I kept up with their journey there, clicking the "care" emoji along with hundreds of other people to let her know that she was not alone.

And then came the day that no parent should ever have to face: the tragic day when her son died.

I wanted to reach out to her, but I didn't know what to say. What could you possibly say? I didn't know her, and she didn't know me. How could a word from a stranger have any impact on her whatsoever in the midst of such devastation?

I could send her a sympathy gift, but I didn't have her address, nor did I have the guts to ask for it. She was grieving, after all. She didn't need to answer a random question from a stranger and give out her home address.

See how easy it is to talk yourself out of extending a hand of care?

We must start this whole "caring for others" thing by recognizing and naming *what is getting in the way* of reaching out to someone who is hurting.

Why is it that we can have someone who means so much to us, who we know is hurting, and we do nothing? Absolutely *nothing*? How is that possible?

I believe it's because we let fear and doubt get in the way and let them paralyze us into inaction. Sometimes these things truly are obstacles that we need to overcome, but many times, my friend, I daresay they are just excuses and reasons we provide for not doing anything.

And that is not okay. Because you know what that means? It means someone might be going through their struggle on their own, without anyone to walk through it with them. It means someone might think that you don't care about them and that they don't matter.

And that is not okay.

It doesn't matter if they are dealing with the loss

of a loved one, a job loss, depression, divorce, a diagnosis, a move, anxiety, or illness... they need people who love them, who care for them, and who will walk through it with them.

So, let's take an honest look at the obstacles that get in the way and the objections we tend to use for not stepping out and taking action in the lives of those who are hurting. In each chapter of this section, we are going to take a closer look at these different obstacles. We're going to identify them, name them, and address them head on.

Are you ready?

Can you identify a time when you *didn't* reach out to a hurting friend for some reason, even though you wanted to? What happened?

_____

_____

_____

_____

Is there a specific situation you're going through right now where you are trying to figure out how to care for a hurting friend? Describe it.

_____

_____

_____

_____

Write out a prayer containing some longings or hesitations you're carrying as you begin reading this book. Are you ready and willing to open your heart up to God? What is your hope as you go through this material? What is your fear?

_____

_____

_____

_____

CHAPTER ONE

Uncertain

> *"Jesus saw the huge crowd as he stepped from the boat, and he had compassion on them and healed their sick." (Matthew 14:14)*

Perhaps the biggest obstacle to reaching out to those who are hurting is that of *uncertainty*. We don't know what to say or do to help our friend feel better. We get so afraid of saying or doing the wrong thing, and we think that we're going to make it worse if we mess up.

We think of all the silly things we've heard people say to us when *we* were the ones who were hurting, and we don't want to be the person who gives the cliché answer—the one who lightheartedly says it's all going to be okay.

Reaching out to a friend who is hurting can feel

like uncharted territory. The uncertainty of what to do or how she'll receive our encouragement can paralyze us, causing us to do nothing when we know we should do something. Because of this, we tend to fade away into the background and leave our friend alone with her grief. We don't call, we don't text, we don't show up at her house or the hospital, and we talk ourselves out of going to the funeral.

As a result, our friend doesn't see us being there for her, because we're *not*.

Let me give you an example. I had a friend who had cancer and she didn't really talk to me directly about it, but I knew she had it. And every time she crossed my path, I felt this nudge to check in with her and see how she was doing. But because I didn't know what to say or how to start the conversation, I just walked on by.

On the day when I finally got up my courage to ask her about how she was feeling, I walked back to where I had previously seen her sitting and she was gone. I had missed my chance.

Has that ever happened to you?

Friend, I don't want us living in regret because we're too afraid to reach out our hand to those in our lives walking through hardship. I want us to break through the fear and reach out anyway. So many people today just walk by those who are hurting and ignore them. I want us to live differently. I want us to not only *notice* them, but also to have the courage to *do* something to help them.

You may be wondering *why*? Why is this so important for us as believers? It's important because God calls us to live in a way that pours His love and compassion onto those around us.

Our key Bible verse for this book is Luke 6:36: "You must be compassionate, just as your Father is compassionate." I invite you to write it down and memorize it, because it shows us that Jesus is our example for loving and caring for those who are hurting. Throughout the New Testament, we see Him showing compassion in so many ways while He was here on earth. One example of Jesus' compassion for people comes from Matthew 14.

It says, "As soon as Jesus heard the news, he left in a boat to a remote area to be alone. But the crowds heard where he was headed and followed on foot from many towns. Jesus saw the huge crowd as he stepped from the boat, and he had compassion on them and healed their sick" (Matthew 14:13-14).

What news did Jesus just hear? That His cousin, John the Baptist, had been killed. Jesus went away to be alone because He was hurting, grieving, and needed some time to perhaps process His emotions. As He was trying to do this, the crowds of people followed Him. He couldn't get away.

And even in His own grief, Jesus had compassion on them. He healed their sick, spent hours teaching them, and then performed the miracle of feeding the 5,000.

What a compassionate Lord we follow.

"You must be compassionate just as your Father is compassionate."

My friend, we are letting fear and uncertainty get in the way of being compassionate and caring for those we see who are hurting.

So, my challenge to you is to just *say something* to that person in your life who is walking through something hard. Say, "I'm so sorry." Say, "I can't imagine what you're going through." Say, "This really stinks." Or if there truly are no words, then just show up and sit beside them. Or give them a hug. Find some way to let your friend know you are there.

It is far better to say *something* and mess it up than to say nothing at all.

Maybe a good place to start today is by taking our key verse, Luke 6:36, and turning it into a prayer: *God, show me what compassion looks like. Show me where I need to be compassionate today. Show me where I'm letting fear get in the way.*

JOURNAL

On a scale of 1 to 10, how much do you struggle with this obstacle of uncertainty?

_____

_____

_____

_____

_____

How does it show up in your life? Name specific situations.

_____

_____

_____

_____

_____

How do you feel when you *don't* acknowledge a friend's hurt/loss/grief?

_____

_____

_____

_____

_____

Read again how Jesus showed compassion in Matthew 14:10-14. What stands out most to you about this passage?

_____

_____

_____

_____

_____

CHAPTER TWO

Unavailable

"Moved with compassion, Jesus reached out and touched him. 'I am willing,' he said. 'Be healed!'"
(Mark 1:41)

As we got started, we discussed why *not* reaching out to people who are hurting is such an issue, and I just want to reiterate some of that again, because I think we need to hear it. I think we really need to understand how much our inaction—our lack of care—can impact the lives of others.

Michael Slater wrote, "To hurt is bad enough, but to hurt alone destroys people physically, mentally, and spiritually." We need to drill that into our hearts and minds.

Have you ever gone through something alone,

with no one there to support you, take care of you, or cry with you? Do you know how devastating it can be?

Just think back over the past few years as we watched hundreds and thousands of people die all alone in hospitals around the world because of the 2020 pandemic. People sitting outside at the hospital because they weren't allowed in to see their wife or their husband. How incredibly heartbreaking. How tragic.

And yet, if we see someone who is hurting, do we take the time to reach out to them, to see how they are doing, to see if we can help? Or do we let fear get in the way? Do we let our questions get in the way?

Again, I'm going to challenge you to take action, because that's what this book is all about. The invitation here isn't only to read the material, but to interact with it by stepping out and *doing something* in the lives of those around you.

In the last chapter, we talked about the first obstacle to reaching out: *uncertainty*. That uncertainty may sound like, "I don't know what to say," or "I don't know what to do." Uncertainty is probably the number one thing that trips us up, because it makes us afraid of saying or doing something that will hurt our friend or be seen as insensitive, and so we say or do nothing at all.

Now we're going to be diving into the second obstacle, which is that you are *unavailable*. In other words, "I don't have the time."

I don't have time to take you to your doctor's appointment.

I don't have time to help you move into your apartment.

I don't have time to watch your kids.

I don't have time to fix you a meal.

I don't have time.

I'm too busy.

I've got too much going on right now.

Can you resonate with this?

Even if you *wanted* to help—which, I'm going to ask you, *do you really want to help?*—you feel like you don't have the time to actually do anything for them.

You're too busy running your kids to school and to practice, too busy getting ready for your meeting, too busy getting to the store, too busy fixing supper, too busy running this committee, and too busy getting volunteers for that...

And friend, you are just. Too. Busy.

Are you really too busy? Or is that just an excuse?

And if you really *are* too busy, is that something God is calling you to change so you can create more margin in your schedule and have the time to be there for your friends when they need you?

I know that so many of us are living at hectic paces, and not only is it destroying us, but it's ruining any chance we have to witness to and care for those in our lives who are really hurting. We don't have time to minister to them because we're too busy doing all these other things.

Are those things really important? Are they things God has called you to do?

I want to invite you to bring those questions before God. Open your calendar or your planner and look at your to-do list. Ask God if there is anything that needs to change. Ask with open hands.

Perhaps for this season, He's okay with you living at this busy pace. You are doing what He has asked you to do. Or maybe you're in a difficult season yourself, caring for an aging parent or taking care of littles at home, and that's exactly where your focus and energy need to be right now. Good for you!

But maybe, just maybe, He will show you one or two things you can let go of so you can reach out to a friend who is going through a really difficult time. So you can let her know how much you care about her. So you can let her know how much she matters to you.

I'll remind you of our key Bible verse for this book, which is Luke 6:36: "You must be compassionate, just as your Father is compassionate." God calls us to show His compassion to the world around us, and Jesus was such a great example for us.

I want to share another story with you where Jesus showed compassion.

In Mark 1, a leper comes up to Jesus, kneels in

front of Him, and begs to be healed. And verse 41 says, "Moved with compassion, Jesus reached out and touched him."

Jesus saw this man's pain, brokenness, and sores, and reached out to physically touch him. In a world that shunned the lepers, cast them out of towns, banished them to live outside of city limits, and didn't let them worship with them in the temple... Jesus, in His compassion, reached out to touch him. And He healed him!

Imagine what that must have been like for the leper to be on the receiving end of such compassion.

Who in your life needs that touch from you? Who needs your attention? Who is hungry for companionship?

"You must be compassionate just as your Father is compassionate."

Don't let fear or unavailability get in the way of caring for those who are hurting. Be like Jesus and reach out. Just reach out.

So, to review, obstacle number one is, *we're uncertain.* "I don't know what to say." "I don't know what to do." I challenged you to just say *something.* As imperfect as it is, let your friend know that you are there for her.

Obstacle number two is that *we're unavailable.* "I don't have the time." This time, I challenged you to look at your calendar and your schedule to see if God is calling you to let go of some things on your plate so that you have more margin and free space in your life to actually be there for your friend: to sit with her, take her to doctor's appointments, or bring her coffee.

We've got three more obstacles to go. Let's keep pressing in.

On a scale of 1 to 10, how much do you struggle with this obstacle of unavailability?

_____

_____

_____

_____

_____

How does it show up in your life? Name specific situations.

_____

_____

_____

_____

_____

How do you feel when you can't show up for a friend who is hurting because you're too busy doing something else?

_____

_____

_____

_____

_____

Read again how Jesus showed compassion in Mark 1:40-43. What stands out most to you about this passage?

_____

_____

_____

_____

_____

CHAPTER THREE

Unfamiliar

"When the Lord saw her, his heart overflowed with compassion. 'Don't cry!' he said." (Luke 7:13)

We are taking an honest look at the obstacles and objections we have that keep us from reaching out to those around us who are hurting and in need of care. In other words, we're looking at what is getting in the way.

What has been your biggest takeaway so far? Or maybe I should ask, what has hit home the most?

I'll be honest, each obstacle is going to get more personal, more honest, and more real as we continue this journey together. As I sat down and really reflected on the comments I've heard people say, at the comments *I* say, to people who are walking through something hard, God opened my eyes to these common obstacles and objections. It's not easy to confess that some of these things come out of my own heart, and I don't like it.

But we have to name them, to call them out, and repent so that we can ask God to help us change.

Are you ready for obstacle number three?

This obstacle is that we are *unfamiliar* with what our friend is experiencing. In other words, "I don't know anything about what my friend is going through."

I've never had cancer before.

I don't have any family members with cancer.

I've never been divorced.

I've never experienced depression.

I've never lost a child before.

I've never been fired from my job.

I've never had to stay in a hospital.

I don't know what they are going through.

I don't know what it's like.

For example, if your friend is struggling with depression, maybe you just don't get it. You've never experienced it before, and you've not had anyone close to you experience it. It's a mystery to you and you don't know how it impacts her daily living. You don't understand how it affects her body. You don't know why she wants to sleep all the time or has to have the lights off. You don't understand why she doesn't just snap out of it and choose to be happy. You simply are not familiar with depression in any way, shape, or form.

So, you either feel unqualified to help her or you're scared by it. It's something new, it's different, and you don't like it because the unfamiliarity of it makes you feel uncomfortable.

The truth is that most, if not all, of us like what's familiar. We'd rather stick with something that is familiar than face something we don't know or understand. In fact, some studies show that people often prefer a familiar option over an unfamiliar one, *even when they know* it's the worst option.

Can you identify with that? Let's look at a couple of more light-hearted examples. You choose to eat at the pizza place you're familiar with, even though their pizza isn't very good, rather than try the place that just opened up down the street and everyone says is delicious. Or, you always take the same route to work every day, so when your route is blocked due to an accident and you have to go a different way without being able to plan for it, it causes you a lot of anxiety.

Familiar things are just more comfortable, which means unfamiliar things are not. We have too much anxiety and too many questions when it comes to something new.

So, how do we break through this obstacle? We take steps to become more familiar with what's unfamiliar.

By simply exposing yourself to the situation or

learning something about it, you can combat your anxiety, which enables you to come alongside your friend. You don't need to know *everything* about what your friend is going through, you just need to know enough to be able to support her.

So instead of being scared or anxious about what feels unfamiliar, be curious: ask questions, do research, and find out the answers.

You could even ask your friend directly the questions you have if she's open to sharing. Some examples might be, "What's it like for you to feel depressed?" "What is a good way for me to help you today?" "What's one thing you wish people knew about depression?"

Or you can research the issue. Find credible website articles about it, read the memoir of someone who went through a similar situation, or listen to a podcast episode where someone is sharing more about it.

As you become more familiar with what your friend is going through, you'll feel more confident in reaching out to her. Again, you don't have to become an expert in the matter. You just need to be aware and show compassion, whether you understand it all or not.

Let's say, for example, that you're not very familiar with hospitals. Maybe they even scare you a little bit, yet a dear friend of yours is in the hospital. What can you do to become more familiar?

You can call ahead and talk to the service counter and ask what room your friend is in, if you don't already know. Ask when visiting hours are, which entrance you should go in, and how to get to your friend's room. Ask if you're allowed to bring anything, like a small gift or book.

When you get there, take your time. Look at the map of the hospital that's either on the wall or on a pamphlet. Figure out how to get to your friend's room and back. Walk slowly and just take in your surroundings as you note what you see.

If it's too much for one trip, plan one visit to the hospital just to look around and then go back again later that day or the next day to actually visit your friend. Take small steps to become more familiar with what's going on, and don't be afraid to ask questions along the way.

We are invited to be compassionate, just as God is compassionate (Luke 6:36). I've already shared a few stories where Jesus demonstrated this for us, and I want to share another one with you now.

It comes from Luke 7:11-15.

> Soon afterward Jesus went with his disciples to the village of Nain, and a large crowd followed him. A funeral procession was coming out as he approached the village gate. The young man who had died was a widow's only son, and a large crowd from the village was with her. When the Lord saw her, his heart overflowed with

compassion. "Don't cry!" he said. Then he walked over to the coffin and touched it, and the bearers stopped. "Young man," he said, "I tell you, get up." Then the dead boy sat up and began to talk! And Jesus gave him back to his mother.

Jesus saw into the lonely life of a widow, a woman who had already lost her husband and who had now lost her only son. She had no family left to care for her or even to live with. When Jesus saw this funeral procession coming out from the village, when He saw the widow herself in her grief and heartache, the Bible says, "His heart overflowed with compassion."

My friend, does your heart overflow with compassion when you see others who are hurting or grieving? Or is it numb? Does their pain even register with you anymore?

"You must be compassionate just as your Father is compassionate."

Ask God to give you a heart of compassion. Ask Him to show you what compassion looks like. Ask Him who in your life needs a bit of compassion today.

We're diving deeper and deeper into the heart of why we don't reach out to help others. I hope and pray that God is speaking to you and inviting you to see how you can take action to care for those around you who are hurting. We've got two more obstacles to go!

On a scale of 1 to 10, how much do you struggle with this obstacle of unfamiliarity?

_____

_____

_____

_____

_____

How does it show up in your life? Name specific situations.

_____

_____

_____

_____

_____

How do you feel when you are faced with an unfamiliar situation?

_____

_____

_____

_____

_____

Read again how Jesus showed compassion in Luke 7:11-15. What stands out most to you about this passage?

_____

_____

_____

_____

_____

CHAPTER FOUR

Uncomfortable

"The LORD is compassionate and merciful, slow to get angry and filled with unfailing love." (Psalm 103:8)

I'm not going to lie, this chapter and the next one are going to be hard. God has really been convicting me of some things in His own gentle, yet firm way. Do you know what I mean, friend?

But we are going to go there. We're going to name it and we're going to ask God to help us change, because our loved ones are worth it, aren't they?

So, obstacle number four is, we are *uncomfortable.*

What does this sometimes look like? "It's hard to watch them struggle."

Is this you? I imagine so. You are here because

you care so deeply. And when others hurt, you hurt, too. You can't help it.

When you see someone crying? Tears start rolling down your face.

When you see someone in pain? Your heart just breaks.

God created us with this amazing sense of empathy. That is by His design. And yet... it's not easy. It's not easy to see someone hurting, to watch them suffer and grieve, or to see the physical toll illness can take on their body.

When a family member has Alzheimer's and they begin to lose their memory, when they begin to call you by the wrong name, when they forget you altogether, when their body begins to shut down... The person caring for them has a thousand little "deaths" as they watch their loved one deteriorate. How incredibly difficult.

To see your friend with cancer for the first time after she has no hair.

To visit a coworker after she has lost a child.

To sit with your dad after he's had a heart attack.

My friend, this is hard stuff. And often, it's the primary caregiver who is there while so many others drift away. It's too hard and uncomfortable.

And so, we stay away.

And when we stay away, we unintentionally send the message that the person hurting doesn't matter to us—that they aren't worth our time and that we don't care.

I'm sure this isn't the message you want to send.

I know it's hard. So, what do we do about this one? What kind of action can we possibly take that will help us overcome this incredibly difficult hurdle?

Friend, we must make a choice. We can choose to harden our hearts so that the suffering of others doesn't bother us, and we just go on our way. Or we can ask God to give us the strength to enter into the suffering with them, to endure, to go to the uncomfortable places, so that we can love them.

When I think about how Jesus responded to the suffering He saw, He repeatedly chose to respond with compassion. Compassion is, in fact, one of the things proclaimed about God throughout Scripture: "The Lord is compassionate and merciful, slow to get angry and filled with unfailing love" (Psalm 103:8; see also Exodus 34:6; Psalm 86:15; Psalm 145:8; Joel 2:13).

The Lord our God is compassionate. And as our Bible verse for this book says, "You must be compassionate, just as your Father is compassionate." Compassionate, for Jesus, wasn't just feeling sorry for the person who was hurting. Compassion always *moved Him into action.*

He *fed* the hungry.

He *touched* the leper.

He *reached out* to the widow.

What is it that compassion is calling you to do?

Where is the uncomfortable place that God is inviting you to step into?

The prayer of my heart is, *God, I pray that You would give me the strength to love others with compassion, even when it is uncomfortable.* May this be your prayer, too.

On a scale of 1 to 10, how much do you struggle with this obstacle of being too uncomfortable?

_____

_____

_____

_____

_____

How does it show up in your life? Name specific situations.

_____

_____

_____

_____

_____

How do you respond when you are uncomfortable, nervous, or anxious?

_____

_____

_____

_____

_____

Read Psalm 103:8 again. What stands out most to you about this verse?

_____

_____

_____

_____

_____

CHAPTER FIVE

Unwilling

"So he complained to the Lord about it: 'Didn't I say before I left home that you would do this, Lord? That is why I ran away to Tarshish!'" (Jonah 4:2a)

As we wrap up our "courageously compassionate" part of the C.A.R.E. framework, we are talking about the most difficult obstacle yet. Are you ready? (*God, help us to have a soft heart so that we can hear the word You have for us here.*)

The fifth obstacle to reaching out to others who are hurting is that we are *unwilling*. In other words, "I don't want to help."

Now, in this case, we are not talking about boundaries, priorities, and when we should step in and when we should not. What this obstacle is all about is that we *very clearly* sense God calling us to do something, to reach out in some way, and we don't want to. We resist, and we dig in our heels instead.

In fact, it reminds me a lot of Jonah.

Jonah had a very clear calling from God to go and proclaim judgment to the Ninevites, which would give them a chance to repent and receive forgiveness, and instead of obeying, he runs in the opposite direction.

The Ninevites were evil, corrupt, and violent, and Jonah didn't want to give them a chance to repent. He didn't want them to experience God's grace and mercy. He saw their evil behavior and passed judgment on them and wanted them to be destroyed.

And yet... God called Jonah to go and give them a chance to repent.

After Jonah finally does so, after he prophesies to those in Nineveh, he sits on a hill nearby and *waits for the city to be destroyed.* That is how hard his heart had grown against the people of Nineveh.

Not only was his heart hard, but he complained to God, "Didn't I say before I left home that you would do this, Lord? That is why I ran away to Tarshish! I knew that you are a merciful and compassionate God, slow to get angry and filled with unfailing love. You are eager to turn back from destroying people" (Jonah 4:2).

Did you catch that? Jonah knew that God was

merciful and compassionate. And God called him to show compassion to the Ninevites by giving them a chance to repent before they were destroyed.

Jonah just didn't want to—he was *unwilling*.

Can you think of a situation where God is calling you to show compassion to someone and you just don't want to? You don't want to extend a hand in welcome. You don't want to forgive. You don't want to give up your time and money to help them. You don't want to visit them in the hospital. You don't want to make time to go to the nursing home.

You just. Don't. Want to.

And so, you don't.

What happens here is twofold: not only is your friend—who needs your compassion—not getting it from you, but you are also running away from God and ignoring Him. That's exactly what the Pharisees did, and Jesus called them out on it. He said, "You are careful to tithe even the tiniest income from your herb gardens, but you ignore justice and the love of God" (Luke 11:42).

John calls us on it, too. In 1 John 3:17-18, he writes, "If someone has enough money to live well and sees a brother or sister in need but shows no compassion—how can God's love be in that person? Dear children, let's not merely say that we love each other; let us show the truth by our actions."

Do we really love each other? We can't just say it.

We actually have to *do* something about it. We must *show* it.

I love the story of Jonah because it's so relatable. Think about it... Jonah himself is the only one who could have told us this story in all its detail. And he doesn't end with some "happily ever after, they all repented and it's all good and I'm amazing" ending. Jonah's story ends with him pouting on the hillside waiting for the city to be destroyed.

And I wonder... how is *your* story going to end? Are you going to be like Jonah, running the opposite way and refusing to reach out to someone who is struggling? Or are you going to trust God and show compassion and care to that person?

This is such a tough obstacle. It's not simply a matter of clearing out more space in our schedule or learning more about what our friend is going through. It's a heart issue. It's about letting God change us, and not all of us are ready for that yet, to be honest, and that's okay. Let's start by asking some questions.

If this is you, if there is something getting in the way of your being willing to reach out, this is what I want you to do: ask God to show you what is getting in the way.

What is causing this unwillingness inside of you? Is it because you don't agree with the person's choices? Is it because you've tried to help before and gotten burned by it? Or maybe you've helped before and the person is right back where they started; your help didn't seem to help at all. Is it because you've been through something similar, and no one helped *you* through it? Are you angry and upset about some other circumstance and you're letting *that* impact how you see *this* situation?

What is causing this unwillingness inside of you? Take some time to sit with that question.

When you're ready, repent. Ask God to help you change. You could say something like this:

"God, I know that there have been times, there might even be times right now, when I just don't want to reach out to someone who is hurting. I know You've called me to. I know You're inviting me to, and I just don't want to do it. There's something inside me that is resisting. And so, I ask that You help me with this, God. Show me what is getting in the way and then give me a new heart. Replace my stubborn heart with a tender, compassionate one. A merciful one, just like Yours."

Luke 6:36 says, "You must be compassionate, just as your Father is compassionate."

God, give us the courage to be compassionate.

On a scale of 1 to 10, how much do you struggle with this obstacle of being unwilling?

_____

_____

_____

_____

_____

How does it show up in your life? Name specific situations.

_____

_____

_____

_____

_____

How does being unwilling to do what God has asked impact other areas of your life?

_____

_____

_____

_____

_____

Read Jonah 4:2 again. What stands out most to you about this passage?

_____

_____

_____

_____

_____

CHAPTER SIX

Which Obstacle Is It for You?

"You must be compassionate, just as your Father is compassionate." (Luke 6:36)

I'm curious, of all the obstacles we've covered, which one has hit home most with you?

Obstacle one: *uncertain*. "I don't know what to say/do."

Obstacle two: *unavailable*. "I don't have the time."

Obstacle three: *unfamiliar*. "I don't know anything about what my friend is going through."

Obstacle four: *uncomfortable*: "It's hard to watch my friend struggle."

Obstacle five: *unwilling.* "I don't want to."

I know I've thought each of these during different situations in my life. They are all things I have experienced and had to work through.

What about you? Which one resonates with you? Are you starting to take action with that obstacle? Are you moving toward breaking through the fear and reaching out anyway?

I don't know about you, but I've had to repent. I've had to ask God to help me with these things, to break through the fear, to trust that He is with me (because He is!). And I know that God doesn't give me a spirit of fear. That's the enemy. I have to take a stand against him. I have to hold on tight to God.

What is amazing to me is how many times throughout Scripture we are told, "Do not fear. Be courageous, because God is with you." My favorite, perhaps, is Isaiah 41:10: "Don't be afraid, for I am with you. Don't be discouraged, for I am your God. I will strengthen you and help you. I will hold you up with my victorious right hand."

God is with you, my friend. He is your God. He will strengthen you. He will help you. He will hold you up. You don't have to do it alone, and you don't have to be afraid.

The next time you go to help a hurting friend, imagine God right there by your side. He is there for you to lean on, to hold your hand, and to guide you in which way to go.

When you are weak, He'll be your strength.
When you are anxious, He'll be your peace.
When you are afraid, He'll be your valor.

Let God's presence give you the courageous compassion you need to care for those around you who are hurting.

Which obstacle hits home most with you? How do you see it show up in your life?

_____

_____

_____

_____

_____

Where do you think this fear came into your life? If you don't know, ask God to reveal it to you.

_____

_____

_____

_____

_____

What is your initial reaction when you see someone who is hurting? Mark all that apply: concerned, heartbroken, frustrated, angry, bitter.

_____

_____

_____

_____

_____

What do you think causes you to react this way? What might it look like for you to respond with courageous compassion instead?

_____

_____

_____

_____

_____

AUTHENTICALLY
TAKING ACTION

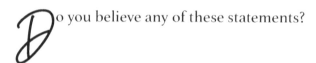o you believe any of these statements?

- Comforters are always warm and fuzzy, touchy-feely, and big huggers.
- Comforters are the ones with whom we have heart-to-heart talks.
- Comforters always know what to say.
- Comforters are always there when people need them.
- Comforters have lots of time to provide enough comfort.

- Comforters are supposed to cheer people up when they are down and tell them to be positive.
- Comforters need to have much in common with the person in distress to be effective.

All of these statements are myths. Val Walker addresses them in her book, *The Art of Comforting*.

The truth is, God has designed each one of us with unique personalities, skills, strengths, gifts, and more. He has also designed us with specific ways that we can demonstrate His kindness, care, and compassion to those around us.

Do you believe that?

The way you encourage and care for others is going to look different than the way I do. And that's okay! In fact, that's good. Because I can't meet everybody's needs, and neither can you.

We each need to know our divine design so we can help others the way God specifically and uniquely created us to.

There are four key areas we are going to explore in this section of the book to discover how God has created you to share His compassion and care with those around you: your characteristics, your skills and training, your experiences, and your personality.

What have you believed about those who encourage, comfort, and care for others? Where did those beliefs come from?

_____

_____

_____

_____

_____

Which of these beliefs are true and which are myths? Mark those that are true with a star.

_____

_____

_____

_____

_____

How do you know those are true and not lies?

_____

_____

_____

_____

_____

CHAPTER SEVEN

Characteristics

"For we are God's masterpiece. He has created us anew in Christ Jesus, so we can do the good things he planned for us long ago." (Ephesians 2:10)

As you discover your divine design, you're going to start by looking at your characteristics. In her book, Val Walker identifies twenty attributes of comforting people. You will not possess all of these, and this is not some sort of checklist to see how many characteristics you can mark off.

It's about identifying how God has wired you to comfort others. *You.* Not me or anyone else.

I'll share Val's attributes and her definition of them here with you, and if you want to learn more,

I highly encourage you to check out her book. She goes into more detail for each one and shares a lot of stories to help you see how they play out. Everything I'm going to share here is just in the first chapter. It's such a good book!

As we go through the list, write down the ones that you feel resonate the most with you. They are meant to be words others would use to describe who you are.

- Present—listens well, gives their full attention, in the moment, focused.
- Empathic—senses the feelings of another person.
- Genuine—sincere and has integrity.
- Respectful—honors people as human beings first and foremost above all roles or status.
- Patient—allows people to move, speak, and think at their own pace; doesn't rush people.
- Caring—kind, compassionate, thoughtful, and considerate.
- Reliable—dependable, trustworthy, will do what they say they will do, and keeps commitments.
- Clear—lets people in distress know what they can realistically do for them, and clarifies their role as comforter, while keeping firm with their boundaries.

- Warm—welcoming, gracious, greets others with a sincere smile, and is approachable.
- Accepting—open-minded, nonjudgmental, receptive, and willing to learn from others.
- Calm—centered, steady, quiet, still, and serene.
- Hopeful—believes that people will find their own way to healing, instills hope without being "preachy" or giving advice.
- Humble—honors his or her own human limitations and vulnerabilities.
- Supportive—offers words, gestures, and actions that build on a person's strengths and preferences, strengths-based.
- Appreciative—grateful, recognizes the value of others, and counts their blessings.
- Generous—giving without expectations, and often spontaneously.
- Gentle/Tender—soft, and can sensitively allow for the other person to respond.
- Adaptable—can respond to changes, is flexible and resourceful, and can go with the flow.
- Wise/Experienced—mature, has life experience, has been through demanding challenges and losses.
- Strong—persevering, resilient, enduring, and confident.

Okay, what words did you write down?

For me, my top five would probably be calm, reliable, gentle, respectful, and caring. Who knew that being a reliable, dependable person could be a way to comfort others?

But let me share why: people who are hurting need people they can count on, don't they? They don't need someone who *says* they're going to take them to their doctor's appointment but then never shows up. They don't need someone who promises to call every week, yet the phone never rings. They need people they can trust—people who can follow through on what they say they're going to do.

It's the same with many of the other characteristics. Sometimes we need to talk to someone who can offer words of wisdom. Sometimes we just need someone to sit in the quiet with us without saying anything at all. Both are good. Both are needed.

So, what comfort and care can you provide to others based on how God has created *you*? What characteristics help you reach out to those who are hurting?

Look over the list of comforting attributes and write down the ones that you feel are authentic for you. If you have trouble choosing, ask your spouse or a good friend for their opinion.

_____

_____

_____

_____

_____

Prayerfully reflect on the ones you marked and highlight your top five.

_____

_____

_____

_____

_____

How can you use these to care for others who are hurting? Brainstorm ideas and be creative!

_____

_____

_____

_____

CHAPTER EIGHT

Skills and Training

"All the women who were skilled in sewing and spinning prepared blue, purple, and scarlet thread, and fine linen cloth. All the women who were willing used their skills to spin the goat hair into yarn." (Exodus 35:25-26)

Now that we've discovered the characteristics God gave you and how those might help you care for others, let's look at your skills. Your skills are things you do that you're good at. It's not a character trait; it's something actionable, something that you do. This can also include your training and expertise.

I want to show you an example here. In Acts 9, we read about a woman named Tabitha. It says that "she was always doing kind things for others and helping the poor" (verse 36). What kinds of things was she doing? A few verses later, we find out.

She made coats and clothes for the widows in her community. That's a very specific skill she had that she used for the benefit of others.

Me? I can't sew very well. I can't make clothes. But I have other skills I can use to help others and care for them during difficult seasons.

For example, when the daughter of a church staff member passed away, I was able to scan in photos of her for the slideshow. Since I knew all the ins and outs of how our copier worked, this was simple for me. Plus, it alleviated some work for the grieving parents and allowed them to focus on what mattered most: being together.

I also think of a friend of mine who was a lawyer. When I was going through my divorce, she walked me through the paperwork and advised me on how to fill things out. She understood the language, the jargon, and how things worked in the legal field. I didn't. It was her training and skill in this area that was incredibly helpful to me during this time.

What are some of the skills that God has given you that you can, in turn, use to care for others? Or what training have you received that could help you support someone else?

Organizing, cleaning, cooking, caring for children, mowing, driving... these are all skills that could easily be used to serve others.

Again, I can't sew, and I'm not very good at cooking. But I'm pretty good with kids and I like to organize things. So, I often let others volunteer for the meal train, and I'll offer to watch the kiddos for a couple of hours.

But there are other skills we have that can also be used to care for others. Skills you may not necessarily think about.

For example, research. If you're good at looking up information and then conveying it to someone else in a way that is easy to understand, that can be so incredibly helpful for someone who is overwhelmed with whatever life has dealt them.

Or what about financial skills? Not everyone can balance a checkbook—or whatever the equivalent is being called these days, since we don't really write a lot of checks anymore. If someone is struggling under the weight of bills and debt, maybe you could offer to sit with them and help them figure out a game plan for making payments in a timely and realistic manner.

Or what about music? So many times in the Bible, we read about how people would play the harp or another instrument, and that music would help someone calm down or sense the Lord's presence. I know there's a specific pianist my daughter and I like to listen to just to be in that calm and relaxed place. It's comforting to us.

Or what about communication? There are many people who would find it beneficial to have a sort of liaison between them and their church family and friends. Someone who could answer everyone's questions so that they could get the rest they need.

Some people, when they are hurting, don't have the bandwidth to respond to every text, every email, or every phone call. They can't find the emotional energy to post on the private church page and share an update about what's going on. But if they could find one person to share that information with who could then pass it along to everyone else... do you have any idea what a blessing that would be to them? Someone trustworthy? Someone who knows what to share and what not to? Someone who doesn't mind answering the phone or posting to the church page? This provides a sort of buffer so the hurting individual can have the space they need to heal.

Or think about being able to translate for someone whose first language is not English. If someone who mostly speaks Spanish is hurt and needs to go to the hospital or talk to their insurance company, having someone they trust who can help translate would provide more confidence and peace in the choices they had to make. And *this* makes an already difficult situation a little bit easier. (Not to mention the blessing of having a friend there with them!)

Or what about art? In Exodus 31:1-7, there were two men (Bezalel and Oholiab) specifically called by God to help build the tabernacle. They were the ones in charge of creating the linens, the ark, and the columns. Are you artistic? If so, how can you use that to minister to others? I know several people who paint inspirational pictures on canvases or as murals in churches. Others craft cards to send to individuals who are lonely or sick.

What other skills can you think of?

I want you to write down the things you are good at—the very actionable skills God has given you and that you have developed over time. Add to that the training that you have received, whether personally or professionally.

You may not be able to see right now how they can benefit someone who is hurting, but I want you to pray and offer those skills to God. Ask Him to show you how you can be a blessing to someone else by using the knowledge and training He has given you.

Identify 5-10 skills you have (even if you don't know right now how you can use them to help others). What would others say you're good at?

_____

_____

_____

_____

_____

What about training? Do you have any certifications, degrees, or licenses that equip you to care for others in a special way?

_____

_____

_____

_____

_____

Read Romans 12:6 and 1 Corinthians 12:7. What do these verses teach us about spiritual gifts? Do you think it applies to what we've talked about in this chapter? Why or why not?

_____

_____

_____

_____

_____

CHAPTER NINE

Experiences

"He comforts us in all our troubles so that we can comfort others. When they are troubled, we will be able to give them the same comfort God has given us." (2 Corinthians 1:4)

After looking at your characteristics and skills, I now invite you to look at the experiences you've had.

You've heard it said, I'm sure, that God uses our story to witness to others. And I am going to echo that here: We can minister to others based on the things we have been through.

For example, I have experience with depression, and I've been through a divorce. So, I can speak to those things a lot more easily than I can something like chronic illness or cancer or job loss, because I haven't experienced those.

Now, if *you've* been through cancer, you'll connect with someone going through cancer. You'll better understand their fears, their anger, and their grief. You'll know the terminology and the treatment. Maybe you'll even know the same hospital and staff. You'll be able to minister to them in a way I never could.

We once had a neighbor who was a little rough around the edges. Without going into details, we knew that he wasn't a particularly safe person. One day, the girl who was staying with him decided she had had enough, and she wanted out, but she didn't have a car. She didn't have a way for her and her daughter to get away.

I didn't know her very well, but she apparently knew me enough to trust me, because one day, I heard a knock at my door, and she asked me if I could drive her and her daughter to her grandma's house in a nearby town.

Immediately, so many thoughts started going through my head. *What if he finds out I helped her? What if she's trying to trick me? I had other plans to do today; if I do this, it's going to take two or three hours.*

But because of my own past experiences and because I had seen enough of the man she lived with to know he wasn't very kind, I agreed. I texted my husband to let him know what was going on and to ask for prayer, and then I helped her leave.

I don't know how your experiences will lead you to help others. Maybe you'll volunteer somewhere at a homeless shelter because you used to be homeless. Maybe you'll help in the schools because that was a safe place for you as a child.

In this case, it was something I physically did to help someone else. But many times, simply sharing my story is comfort enough.

Now, I don't share my story with everyone. Instead, I've chosen to share my story personally with others who are walking similar roads. It can be a private, intimate conversation where I'm trusting someone with my story in hopes that they will be encouraged in theirs. We can talk about the specific details, explore all the feelings, and discuss specific steps they can take to move forward or take care of themselves.

You may want to share your story publicly. Maybe God is inviting you to be more open with it. That's great! Go for it. Or, like me, share it one-on-one with those who are struggling in the same way you have struggled.

The bottom line is that God uses our experiences to encourage others. "He comforts us in all our troubles so that we can comfort others. When they are troubled, we will be able to give them the same comfort God has given us" (2 Corinthians 1:4).

Go ahead and jot down the main experiences that come to mind where you have struggled but overcome. Even the ones you are still dealing with today.

In your journal, you'll be able to explore these some more. But for now, simply recognize that these experiences equip you to connect with someone else in a way that I cannot. And that is a part of your divine design, my friend.

Write down 1-3 experiences you've had, ones you might be able to use to help others going through similar things. These are often (but not always) the harder places of our lives.

_____

_____

_____

_____

_____

Which part of your story is easiest to share with others? Which part scares you the most? Why?

_____

_____

_____

_____

_____

When has someone shared their story with you and encouraged you through a difficult season?

_____

_____

_____

_____

CHAPTER TEN

Personality

"You made all the delicate, inner parts of my body and knit me together in my mother's womb." (Psalm 139:13)

My church has recently started leading a Bingo game at a local senior living community a couple of times a month, and I'll admit, I was pretty nervous to join in. But doing something with a group of friends is a lot easier than doing it on your own, so I brushed my anxiety aside and showed up anyway.

The first week, we were introduced to a man named Bill. He was deaf and needed someone to write the Bingo numbers down for him so he could play along.

I immediately volunteered for the job. As a pretty high introvert, this gave me a meaningful job to do without needing to make a lot of small talk, which can be so incredibly draining. In fact, I really didn't have to talk at all. But I sure did smile a lot and support him as he played the game!

Our personality can have a big impact on the way we desire to come alongside others who are hurting. And there are a *multitude* of personality tests out there. Feel free to dive into the one you resonate with the most.

The one I'm partial to is the Myers-Briggs Type Indicator (MBTI). It expands on the differences between introverts and extraverts (which is *huge* in how we interact with those around us), but it also offers insight into other areas that are helpful to us here. The MBTI helps us identify our preferences in four different areas of our personality:

- How we receive and use our energy.
- How we take in information.
- How we make decisions.
- How we approach the outside world.

Understanding our preferences in these areas can help us with things like working with others, dealing with conflict, finding time to recharge, and making wise choices.

Having taken the assessment, I know my MBTI

type is INFJ (though I'm very close on the T/F spectrum). Don't worry too much about the letters. This is what my letters tell me:

- I need a *lot* of time alone to recharge.
- I like quiet spaces.
- I often use my intuition to gather information, but I also like to dig into some research.
- I rarely like surprises. (Ask me about the time someone threw me a surprise party.)
- I'm not good at sharing my own feelings, but I can be pretty good at picking up on the feelings of others.
- Relationships are important to me.
- I like to schedule things out and know what is coming.
- I prefer clean spaces, but a little mess doesn't bother me.

Pick your preferred personality assessment or just think about what you know to be true about yourself and write it out. Not in a superior or even a judgmental way, but in a naming sort of way, as if to say, "This is who I am." Recognize your strengths and weaknesses and see how you can authentically serve a friend who is going through a difficult season.

Going to a big fundraiser or event in support of disease awareness isn't something that naturally draws my interest. But if I have a dear friend who is struggling with that disease, I'd more authentically be able to sit with her one-on-one or offer to drive her to doctor's appointments or something to that effect. (And preferably, I would have it on my calendar and know it's coming rather than get a last-minute, "Can you take me to my appointment right now?" kind of call.)

It also lets me know that I need to block off time to recharge after helping someone else. I love them dearly and enjoy being able to help! But once that is done, it's best for me to go home and relax rather than run and do something else.

How does *your* personality impact the way you show up for others?

What do you know to be true about your personality? Name things as specifically as you can—without judging yourself!

If you know your type from any of the personality models, go ahead and write it here. Feel free to research these a bit if it interests you.

Looking at your personality, how can you then more authentically reach out to others who are hurting? What is important for you to know or remember?

CHAPTER ELEVEN

Your Divine Design

"God has given each of you a gift from his great variety of spiritual gifts. Use them well to serve one another." (1 Peter 4:10)

How has God designed you to encourage, comfort, and care for those around you? Take a look at the things you wrote down in each chapter: your characteristics, skills, experiences, and personality.

For example, here's what *my* divine design might look like:

Characteristics: calm, reliable, gentle, respectful, caring.

Skills and Training: organized, administrative, research, artistic, writing, caring for kids.

Experiences: depression, divorce, ministry.

Personality: INFJ.

What does *yours* look like? Do you see how God might be inviting you to use these things to reach out to those around you?

Does any of it scare you?

Talking about those hard places in my life is never any fun. Yet I have seen God use those hard places to minister to other women who are crushed, overwhelmed, and feeling defeated.

And I'm not going to lie, there are still plenty of times I get jealous of the way God has wired others to provide comfort and care. They are more sociable, able to make women feel accepted and welcome, and know when to put up boundaries about what they can and cannot provide.

It's then I must remind myself that God has wired me this way for a reason. My quiet companionship might be exactly what my overwhelmed friend needs. My ability to research options and lay it out in a way that is easy to understand might help them cut through the confusion and make the best decision for them. My experience with depression might give them insight into why they are feeling that way or provide ideas for how they can make it through the next day.

We need the entire body of Christ here. Because I'm not enough on my own, and neither are you. We need everyone working together, offering their special type of care, to make sure no one is alone through a difficult season.

So, continue to pray for the courage to reach out, care, share your story, or volunteer your services. God will be there to guide you and help you along the way.

Review what you've learned about yourself in this section. What is *your* divine design?

_____

_____

_____

_____

_____

When you look over your characteristics, skills, experiences, and personality, can you see how these things can be used to comfort and care for others? Take time to explore the possibilities.

_____

_____

_____

_____

Do you feel you are stewarding your gifts, skills, and experiences well?

_____

_____

_____

_____

Look up 1 Peter 4:10 in your Bible and copy it in your journal. How is God speaking to you through this verse?

_____

_____

_____

_____

_____

R

RELYING
ON GOD

We know that God has commanded us to be compassionate, just as the Father is compassionate (Luke 6:36).

He tells us to love our neighbor.

He tells us to care for the orphans and widows.

He tells us to grieve with those who grieve.

He tells us to take care of the poor.

But how? How do we do all these things in a way that is healthy and honoring to Him?

The truth is, we need to let God be the one to guide us in how and when to reach out to others. Because, while the general command is clear—be compassionate, loving, and caring—the specific way it plays out for each of us will be different.

Are all of us called to go overseas and be missionaries? No.

Are all of us called to be foster parents? No.

Are all of us called to teach Sunday school? No.

We can't be in all the places. You would wear yourself out trying to visit all the nursing homes and all the hospitals and all the shut-ins from church and all those who are sick at home and all the kids who need a caring adult in their lives and all those who are in jail... There's only so much of you to go around.

So how do you decide where and how to reach out to others? You must let God guide you.

As I have prayed about this in my own life, I have received pretty clear direction from God about where my care is focused right now. It doesn't mean it won't change, but for this season of my life, I know who my people are. I know who I'm reaching out to. I know who I'm focused on.

And God will reveal that to you, too.

But in order to receive that from Him, you have to be able to hear God's voice, recognize His presence, and sense those sacred nudges from Him inviting you to reach out and do something even when you're a little scared to do so.

This is known as the practice of discernment.

And friend, I want you to know that God *wants* us

to hear His voice. He's not intentionally speaking in a way that you will not understand. No, He says that His sheep know His voice.

So let God teach you what His voice sounds like, and then let Him guide you into knowing who you can help and how He wants you to do it. We'll learn how to do this in three specific ways in this section: the sacred echo, recognizing how God speaks to you, and a spiritual practice called the Examen.

Do you feel like anything gets in the way of your hearing from God during this season of your life?

_____

_____

_____

_____

_____

What practices do you currently have in place to hear from God and spend time with Him?

_____

_____

_____

_____

_____

Read Psalm 27:8. What does this verse tell us about God's desire to talk with us?

_____

_____

_____

_____

_____

CHAPTER TWELVE

Why We Need Discernment in Caring for Others

"If you need wisdom, ask our generous God, and he will give it to you. He will not rebuke you for asking." (James 1:5)

Think about the questions you have when someone you care about is hurting:

- How do I know how God is leading me to help others?
- My friend seems to be having a hard time. How do I know whether to approach her about it or not?

- What do I say to loved ones who are hurting?
- When do I say "yes" to helping someone and when do I need to let *others* be the ones to help instead?

I know there are books and articles out there that will tell you, "Say this, don't say that." "Do this, don't do that." But the truth is, what is helpful for *one* person isn't necessarily helpful for *another*. And to make it even more difficult, saying one thing at one moment in time could be hurtful, but saying it a few weeks or even days later is just what they needed to hear.

Plus, there are times when we help others out of love only to realize our "help" wasn't helpful at all. Maybe we even made it worse.

I have learned that we must develop discernment so we can let God be the one to guide us in caring for our friends.

Discernment is being able to recognize God's presence and voice. We often seek God's guidance for the "big moments" and decisions of our lives, and we forget that He cares about the everyday, ordinary moments, too. He can meet us in those places and speak to us there.

It's not just about hearing from Him, but learning to see His fingerprints on the situations in our lives and the work He is doing in our hearts and in the hearts of others.

What we're doing is building up muscle, so to

speak. We practice hearing from God daily so that we can seek Him in those specific situations we encounter every day, such as:

Do we give to the beggar on the side of the road?

Do we invite our friend out for coffee?

Do we cut out other things so we have time to babysit our friend's kids?

Do we say "God bless" to the cashier?

I was at the dentist's office just the other day and my hygienist had Christian music playing in the background. It was such a welcome playlist compared to other medical offices we had been in recently that played songs I didn't want my kids to be singing.

While I was sitting there, I felt the nudge to tell her I appreciated it. So, I did. And she was encouraged because I dared to say something.

I could have simply gone about my day without saying anything at all. No one was hurting or struggling (that I knew of). There was no intentional prayer asking for guidance. But it was a prompting from the Lord to speak an encouraging word to her.

And that's where it all usually starts: with the small things. Luke 16:10 tells us, "If you are faithful in little things, you will be faithful in large ones. But if you are dishonest in little things, you won't be honest with greater responsibilities."

So, let's start small by recognizing simple (but powerful!) ways God speaks to us and how we respond to those invitations from Him. Over time, we'll be able to sense His promptings in larger things that take a little more courage on our part.

Where do you struggle with discerning God's voice?

_____

_____

_____

_____

_____

What questions are you holding before God right now? What do you want to know?

_____

_____

_____

_____

_____

Is there a particular situation where you struggle to know how to respond? Go ahead and name that before the Lord and see what He might have to say to you.

_____

_____

_____

_____

CHAPTER THIRTEEN

Hearing the Sacred Echo

"As iron sharpens iron, so a friend sharpens a friend." (Proverbs 27:17)

You might think, "God doesn't speak to me," and I'm going to challenge you to rethink that. To begin challenging that thinking, we're going to talk about sacred echoes.

Margaret Feinberg describes the sacred echo as a time when you hear a word, phrase, or idea from multiple places in a short amount of time. Has that ever happened to you?

There have been times when I read something in a book that was then repeated on a podcast, which was then repeated by a friend. Those are sacred echoes.

One time, it was all about shame and how Jesus carried that to the cross with Him. Earlier this year, it was about unhurried living and being present in the moment. Most recently, it has been about being willing to do the uncomfortable things so I can grow.

Maybe for you, the image of a tree standing strong in a storm comes to mind. You hear Jeremiah 17:8 on the radio: "They are like trees planted along a riverbank, with roots that reach deep into the water. Such trees are not bothered by the heat or worried by long months of drought. Their leaves stay green, and they never stop producing fruit."

The next day, you receive a card from a friend with a big, mature tree on the front, so wide that you know it has been around for centuries, and there just happens to be a river off in the distance.

As you take a walk along a local trail, you can't help but notice all the trees lining the riverbank, and how some are standing strong while others look like they could fall over if you pushed it with your little finger.

That, my friend, is a sacred echo. Maybe it leads you to ponder which one best describes you. Are you a strong tree? Have you planted your roots down deep into the soil? Are you bearing fruit and staying alive even when circumstances around you get hard?

There's another type of sacred echo, though. One I don't like to get. You see, sometimes I receive these sacred echoes from God because I fail to act the first time.

Maybe I sense that He wants me to reach out to a certain friend of mine I know is hurting, and I acknowledge it's a good idea, but I never do anything about it. A few days later, He brings that person's name to mind again and reminds me about it. I'm too busy to do anything right that second, so I write it in my planner and keep moving.

This happens again and again until I finally obey what He is asking me to do!

Take a few minutes and write down as many sacred echoes as you can think of in your own life. If you can remember specific words and phrases, write those down, too. If you're having trouble remembering, ask God to bring those situations to mind.

Continue this practice in the days and weeks ahead, as long as God leads you to do so. As an experience comes to mind, add it to your list. Consider starting a journal where you can keep record of God's speaking to you, especially these sacred echoes. You can jot down the phrase or lesson that comes to mind, along with where you heard it: a song, a book, a friend, the Bible. Then maybe take a sentence or two and reflect on what you sense God is inviting you to do with it.

The sacred echo is just one amazing way God speaks to us. Let's look at some others in the upcoming chapter!

What do you think about the idea of sacred echoes? Have you experienced them before?

_____

_____

_____

_____

_____

Make a list of specific times you remember sensing these echoes from God. What word, phrase, or idea did He repeat to you?

_____

_____

_____

_____

_____

God can work through everyday, ordinary situations to speak to His people. Have you experienced this in any way?

_____

_____

_____

_____

_____

CHAPTER FOURTEEN

Recognizing God's Voice

"I am the good shepherd; I know my own sheep, and they know me." (John 10:14)

In addition to the sacred echo, we also want to learn how to recognize God's voice, and we're going to start with a Bible story. It's probably one that you've heard before, because it's one that is referenced a *lot* when it comes to hearing God's voice. But I want to show you something that most people don't talk about or maybe don't notice.

It's the story of Elijah. Let's read 1 Kings 19:9-13.

But the Lord said to him, "What are you doing here, Elijah?"

Elijah replied, "I have zealously served

the Lord God Almighty. But the people of Israel have broken their covenant with you, torn down your altars, and killed every one of your prophets. I am the only one left, and now they are trying to kill me, too."

"Go out and stand before me on the mountain," the Lord told him. And as Elijah stood there, the Lord passed by, and a mighty windstorm hit the mountain. It was such a terrible blast that the rocks were torn loose, but the Lord was not in the wind. After the wind there was an earthquake, but the Lord was not in the earthquake. And after the earthquake there was a fire, but the Lord was not in the fire. And after the fire there was the sound of a gentle whisper. When Elijah heard it, he wrapped his face in his cloak and went out and stood at the entrance of the cave.

And a voice said, "What are you doing here, Elijah?"

First, let's note that Elijah doesn't seem to have a problem hearing from God, since God asks him a question and he answers. He already knew what God sounded like. He heard God's voice.

Then, notice it says, "God wasn't in the windstorm." Okay, I have a question for you: has God ever revealed Himself through the wind before?

Yes! In Exodus 10:13 and 19, we see that God used the wind to bring in the plague of locusts and to blow them back out. In Exodus 14:21, He used the wind to push back the Red Sea. In Numbers 11:31, God used the wind to bring quail to the Israelites out in the wilderness.

God *had* revealed Himself through the wind before.

Again, it says, "God wasn't in the earthquake." Had He ever revealed Himself through an earthquake before?

Yes! In Exodus 19:18, God descended from the mountain and the whole mountain shook violently. In Numbers 26:10, the earth opened up and swallowed Korah and his family in judgment for his sin.

Those sound like earthquakes to me.

It says, "God wasn't in the fire." Had He ever revealed Himself through fire before?

Yes! We have the burning bush in Exodus 3:2, the pillar of fire in Exodus 13:21-22, and God coming in the form of a fire in Exodus 19:18. We also have the glory of the Lord appearing like fire in Exodus 24:17 and fire blazing forth from the Lord's presence in Leviticus 9:24, Leviticus 10:2, and Numbers 16:35. Not to mention that Deuteronomy 4:24 refers to God as a devouring fire!

All three (wind, earthquake, fire) were ways God

had previously revealed Himself to His people. *He just didn't use those ways here with Elijah!*

Does God speak in a gentle whisper? Absolutely. But He has so many other ways to speak to us, as well.

- Dreams
- Visions
- Thunder
- Clouds
- Creation/Nature
- His Word
- Art
- Music
- Books

How does God speak to *you*?

In your journal, you'll have a place to write down all the times you remember when you knew, beyond a shadow of a doubt, that God was speaking to you. In it, I want you to record what you heard from Him and how you heard it. Was it through His Word? Was it through a friend?

God is so creative, and He speaks to us in a way that we can understand. So, pay attention to the ways He normally shows up in your life, but don't limit yourself to those. He can start speaking to you in new and different ways.

What have you been taught about God's voice and how He interacts with His people?

_____

_____

_____

_____

_____

Do you need to revisit any of these ideas or let go of them altogether? Is there anywhere you want to do further study of God's Word to see what He says about this?

_____

_____

_____

_____

_____

Make a list of every time you know, beyond a shadow of a doubt, that you've heard from God or sensed His presence with you. Be as specific as you can—where you were, how you heard/sensed Him, any message He gave you, etc. If you struggle to think of anything, ask God to bring these occasions to mind.

_____

_____

_____

_____

_____

Do you see any patterns or themes when it comes to *how* God speaks to you? (For example, is it usually through the Bible? A friend? Nature? Music?)

_____

_____

_____

_____

_____

Is there a specific physical location where you most sense God's presence? If so, where?

_____

_____

_____

_____

_____

CHAPTER FIFTEEN

Practicing the Examen

"If you look for me wholeheartedly, you will find me." (Jeremiah 29:13)

There's one exercise in particular I want to share with you that will help you grow in discernment (and remember, discernment is learning to recognize God's voice and His movement in your life).

And it is the practice of the Examen.

Now, Examen is just a fancy word for examining or reflection. This is typically something we do at the end of the day, so we can look back and reflect on what has happened, but really, you can do it anytime.

Trevor Hudson says that we learn not from our experiences, but from our *reflection* upon those experiences, and the Examen is simply that: a reflection upon our experiences. We are going to be looking at where God has been present throughout our day. We're going to be looking for His fingerprints.

There are several ways to practice the Examen. You can find the more traditional version online, but I've adapted it for my own use and have shared some ideas below. All of these are great to use with kids, so feel free to practice it with your family, too!

The first is what I call Kindful, Thankful, Joyful, Prayerful.

Kindful: Where did you see kindness today? Look back through your day and identify very specific situations where you saw kindness.

Thankful: What are you thankful for today? Again, be specific.

Joyful: Where did you experience joy today? What brought a smile to your face or laughter to your lips?

Prayerful: What (or who) do you want to bring before God in prayer and petition?

The idea behind this is that anytime we see kindness, can express our thanks to God, or experience joy, those are all places where God is moving, even though it may not seem like it. As we recognize where those things show up in our lives, we can see where God is moving and interacting with us.

The second form of the Examen is very similar, but this time, we're going to look for the fruit of the Spirit.

Where did you see patience today?

Where did you see goodness?

Where did you see faithfulness?

Where did you see self-control?

As fruit of the Spirit, we know that when we see these things—in our lives or in the lives of those around us—we are seeing where God has been planting and watering His seeds. These are not things we can do on our own. God is at work, and when we see His fruit, we know He is there.

Another way to practice the Examen is to remember that Jesus is the Way, the Truth, and the Life. And so, in this one, we reflect on questions like:

Where did I see or hear something true? Because Jesus is the truth, anytime we hear the truth, we are experiencing God.

Where did I receive life? Because Jesus is the life, we know that when we receive life, we're receiving it from God. We can only receive life from things that are godly.

I invite you to pick one of those sets of questions and use it every night to look back at your day and see where God is at work. You'll begin to sense where He is moving in your life, and it will open your ears and heart to better hear His voice as He speaks to you.

Which version of the Examen resonates most with you? Why does this one speak to you right now?

_____

_____

_____

_____

_____

At what point in the day will you practice the Examen (morning, noon, evening, bedtime)?

_____

_____

_____

_____

_____

How will you practice the Examen? (In private, prayerful reflection? Writing it out and recording it in your journal or planner? Verbally answering the questions with your spouse or friend or family?)

_____

_____

_____

_____

CHAPTER SIXTEEN

Recognizing God's Invitation to Reach Out

"Your own ears will hear him. Right behind you a voice will say, 'This is the way you should go,' whether to the right or to the left." (Isaiah 30:21)

Remember, the *reason* we practice hearing God's voice (besides getting to know Him more intimately) is so we can begin to sense those nudges from Him as to when to reach out to a friend, how He wants us to schedule our week, what words to write on a card, etc.

There was a lady who had several health issues and who was losing her eyesight. I didn't know her very well at all, yet had visited her with a friend.

When I heard that one of the things she missed the most was being able to read the Bible on her own, I almost instantly felt that nudge in my spirit (you know the one).

I thought about the audio/CD Bible I had in my car. I liked to listen to it during some of my longer drives. Yet in this instance, I knew I was being invited to pass it along to her instead. It was a nudge from God that I had come to know because I had learned to recognize His voice.

I also think about the time when I was completely exhausted and worn out and then my phone started ringing. I decided in my mind to not answer it, knowing I needed the rest. While that's okay on many occasions (please hear me that the need for rest is okay!), this was a time when God asked me to answer the phone anyway. It ended up being someone who needed a ride.

It was then that I relied on 1 Peter 4:11: "Do you have the gift of helping others? Do it with all the strength and energy that God supplies." I took a deep breath, asked for God's help, picked up my purse, and went to pick her up.

The truth is, she didn't have anyone else to call in that moment. She felt bad for bothering me, and I assured her she wasn't a bother and I was happy to help. It was a chance to minister to her when she was in a difficult situation.

My husband often senses when people need help

with food or groceries. His years of experience in grocery store management has given him a good awareness for this. But even more important than that, he knows when he senses that nudge from God to help pay for someone's food at the store, and he listens. I'm never surprised when I get a text message from him sharing that he helped someone else.

How do *you* sense God's nudge to help? What does it feel like?

Now, friend, I'll be honest: there are times when I sit down to write a card to a friend, and I don't feel any particular inspiration from the Holy Spirit, so I just write a message. Afterward, I've had a friend tell me it's exactly what she needed to hear, down to the verse that I "just happened" to include.

God can be working in you and through you *without you even realizing it*. But it's as we practice hearing His voice and seeking His presence that we can intentionally seek Him for guidance in how to reach out and care for our friends.

God will let you know when to reach out, and He will also let you know when to stand back and let someone else help. If we're not gifted in a particular area, we can take away the ability of those who *are* gifted to use that in service to others. It's okay to step back and let others move forward.

Plus, there are times when our hurting friend needs to take action on their own. Because sometimes our help actually *hinders* someone from taking a step they need to take.

There are also seasons of service and seasons of rest. We need God to guide us here!

Has God ever nudged you to reach out to someone before? If so, how? What did He invite you to do?

_____

_____

_____

_____

_____

Have you ever ignored this prompting from God? What made you do so?

_____

_____

_____

_____

_____

Look up Isaiah 30:21 in your Bible and copy it in your journal. How is God speaking to you through this verse?

_____

_____

_____

_____

_____

E

EVER MINDFUL OF
THE OTHER PERSON

Once upon a time, I was a college public speaking instructor. I always gave a sample speech to help my students have some idea of what I was looking for in their presentations. It was the same speech every time: social isolation.

I shared how dangerous isolating yourself from others can be, incorporating stories from my own life when I struggled with depression. And just about every semester, a handful of students would approach me and tell their own stories. I was honored to bear witness to the experiences they shared.

But the way I responded to an eighteen-year-old girl was different from the way I responded to a forty-six-year-old man. Both students in my class, but both with incredibly different backgrounds and personalities.

And *that's* what we're going to talk about in this section: how to tailor our response to our friend. You see, this encouragement thing is not all about us; it's about *showing love to our friend.*

As we think about caring for those who are hurting, we can't be selfish in the use of our gifts, which are given to us in order to build up the body. And we can't say, "It's not my personality." We need to take into consideration our friend's needs and preferences and figure out what would be truly helpful and meaningful to her, not just what is easy for us.

I've had to do this as a more introverted person. Some things aren't comfortable for me. But out of love, I stretch myself to serve my friend anyway.

Again, there are several areas we can think through as we reflect on how to best support our friend in this situation. We're going to start with the needs our friend has already expressed clearly, then we're going to move into our friend's love languages and personality, and finally, we'll talk about how our relationship with her impacts what we choose to do.

Each situation is unique when it comes to caring for a friend, which means there is no specific script to follow. What is good about that? What is difficult?

_____

_____

_____

_____

_____

Read 1 Corinthians 13. How does this relate to comforting and caring for others?

_____

_____

_____

_____

Sometimes we must put our gifts, skills, and experiences aside and just serve our friend out of love, whether or not it "fits" us. How do you feel about that?

_____

_____

_____

_____

What kind of attitude do you have when it comes to caring for your friend—especially when it isn't in a way that comes naturally to you?

_____

_____

_____

_____

_____

CHAPTER SEVENTEEN

Expressed Needs

"Do not withhold good from those who deserve it when it's in your power to help them." (Proverbs 3:27)

There are a lot of times when we overcomplicate things. We scratch our heads and wonder what in the world we can do for our friend when the answer is right there in front of us.

That's why we're starting this section with your friend's expressed needs. During this difficult season, what has she asked for? What needs or frustrations has she communicated to you?

When I was in the hospital after giving birth to my son, I noticed that the tissues provided were making my nose incredibly red and sore. So, when my mom asked if there was anything she could bring or do for us, I immediately said, "Soft Kleenexes!" It was a simple request and perhaps a small comfort, but it meant so much to me.

Your friend might be able to name what she needs from you. You might also be able to glean it from your conversations with her.

Let's say your friend is taking care of an aging parent, but she also has small children at home. As you talk with her, she mentions her struggle to be present with her kids with all the attention she must give to her parent. She is also too tired to cook a meal for supper, so she's constantly grabbing take-out and bringing it home.

Right there, you see that she could probably use a bit of a break from her caregiving responsibilities so she can spend some quality time with her kids. Would you be able to sit with her parent for an hour or so? This would free her up so she can get out of the house and enjoy being present with her kids. Maybe you could also bring supper over so they could just put it in the crockpot and have it ready when they sit down to eat.

Don't overlook the things that are already so clear.

While ideally, you could volunteer for things that are authentic to you—things we identified back in section two—you may need to step out and do something that *doesn't* quite fit in your wheelhouse. But do your best to meet her where she's at.

Remember, this is about *her*, not you. So, if someone needs to bend, it needs to be you.

Let me put this in a different light. When I was struggling with depression back in college, many times, friends would encourage me to go out to a restaurant or event with them. They assumed being around other people would help cheer me up.

However, what I *really* needed was a quiet space to be alone or just to sit with one dear friend in companionable silence. All the noise and activity from being around others only made me feel worse. And when I politely declined their invitations, there were times they chose to "bring the party" to me instead.

I know these friends cared about me dearly. I know they were trying to help me. And yet... I didn't feel like my feelings or desires mattered. They failed to take my expressed needs into consideration.

Realize, too, that sometimes expressed needs means stating clearly what you do *not* need.

So, let me ask you this: has your friend communicated boundaries in any way? Has she asked for privacy or space? Maybe cooking is one way she copes with stress, so the offer of a meal train isn't something she wants to accept. Maybe her family just lost a loved one and she doesn't *want* to be away from her kids right now, so the invitation to babysit isn't a good fit.

Maybe your friend doesn't know *what* she needs, but she knows very clearly what she does *not* need.

Honor that.

Don't force your help on her just to make yourself feel better. It is far more helpful and loving to listen to what your friend tells you she needs—and *does not* need—and respond appropriately.

This is the best place to start, my friend.

Has your friend communicated any needs clearly? If so, write them down. If not, reflect on conversations you've had with her. What might you be able to glean from those chats about what she does (or does *not*) need?

_____

_____

_____

_____

_____

Is it hard for you to *not* do something your friend has asked you not to do? For example, if she asks for space, is it hard for you to give her space?

_____

_____

_____

_____

Have you ever had anyone ignore or overlook your clearly expressed desires before? How did that make you feel?

_____

_____

_____

_____

_____

CHAPTER EIGHTEEN

Love Languages

"No one has ever seen God. But if we love each other, God lives in us, and his love is brought to full expression in us." (1 John 4:12)

A second way we can provide meaningful care to our friend is to look at her love languages. Love languages indicate how we receive love and care from others.

We don't want to identify our *own* love languages because it's not about us, right? We need to pay attention to our friend and try to figure out what *her* love language is.

The love languages are from Dr. Gary Chapman, and through his research, he identified five primary ways we receive love from those around us, especially our spouses and close friends:

- Words of Affirmation—using words to encourage and affirm.
- Acts of Service—demonstrating love through action.
- Quality Time—spending meaningful time together.
- Gifts—receiving a special present.
- Physical Touch—receiving appropriate and caring touch.

(Interestingly enough, these five love languages have been adapted to the five languages of appreciation in the workplace—ways to *encourage* your coworkers or staff.)

If you're new to the five love languages, it might help to start with identifying your own. How do you prefer to receive love from your husband, best friend, or parent? Do you like backrubs? Small souvenirs from their trips? Someone to help clean the house? Running errands together? Handwritten birthday or anniversary cards? What makes you feel appreciated and cared for?

Now it's time to identify your *friend's* primary love language. If nothing jumps out at you right away, you can look at what she asks for most often.

- Is she constantly asking for a coffee date? She probably leans toward quality time. She enjoys spending one-on-one time with you!
- Does she ask you to watch her kids for an hour? She values acts of service and appreciates having some extra help.
- Does she give you a big hug every time she sees you? Her love language is probably touch. Hugs and being close together mean a lot to her.
- Does she send you a lot of text messages? Words of affirmation speak volumes to her. She needs to hear how much you care about her.

We tend to naturally show our love for others using our *own* love language, so watch how she interacts with you or those around her.

Once you know her love language, you can use that to help you brainstorm ways to reach out.

For example, if her love language is words of affirmation, obviously sending her a card, text, or letter would be very meaningful ways to reach out to her. But you can also think about texting her a joke, emailing her a favorite memory of yours, or sending her a voice message with a prayer. Those are all ways you can use words of affirmation to reach out to her and let her know you care.

Or what if her love language is acts of service?

You could do things like clean her house or mow her yard. But don't be afraid to think outside the box. Maybe you could use your home as a sort of "day retreat" and let her spend the day there to get away for a while and take a break. Or you might cook her a meal or run errands for her.

Take the time to study your friend and discover what her primary love language is. Then pray about how you can intentionally show love and care to her in *that* way during this difficult season in her life.

JOURNAL

How does your friend naturally show love and care
to those around her? (Think about how she interacts
with her spouse, kids, and close friends.)

_____

_____

_____

_____

_____

What love language do you think is her primary love
language? Feel free to pick her top two if you can't decide.

_____

_____

_____

_____

_____

How might you show your friend that you care about
her using these love languages? Brainstorm as many
ideas as you can!

_____

_____

_____

_____

_____

CHAPTER NINETEEN

Personality and Preferences

*"If I gave everything I have to the poor and even
sacrificed my body, I could boast about it; but if I
didn't love others, I would have gained nothing."
(1 Corinthians 13:3)*

So first, you are going to look at your friend's expressed needs. Second, you're going to try to
identify her primary love language. Third, you
also want to consider your friend's personality and
preferences.

We are all wired so differently. Some are introverts, some extraverts. Some like surprises, some
don't. And some like things organized while others
could care less. We talked about this back in section
two, but for that, we focused on *your* personality. Now

we're going to look at your *friend's*. As you brainstorm ways to help your friend, you want to use *her* personality and preferences as a sort of filter.

For example, your friend is a words of affirmation gal. She also loves being around people. So, taking a moment during the church service to recognize her and affirm the work that she is doing, even to pray over her and her situation, would be something she would probably love!

But if your friend is on the more introverted side, she needs to receive her words of affirmation in a different way: through a handwritten note, a text message, or a private conversation off to the side where others can't hear.

Does she like surprises? Would she enjoy an impromptu gathering of her closest friends or would that cause her too much stress?

You can either think about your friend's personality test results if you know them or just think about what you already know about her.

Does she like to have a lot of people in her home or not?

Is she more public or private in her personal life?

Does she have a schedule and routines she likes to live by?

Is she up early in the morning or does she like to stay up late at night?

You can revisit chapter 10, only this time, keep your friend in mind instead of yourself. Again, there are a *lot* of personality assessments available. She might have shared this with you in the past or you might be able to figure it out by reading through the various personality types within any given model.

You can even think about her favorites: favorite food or restaurant, favorite coffee and coffee shop, favorite author or book series, favorite place to go and relax, and favorite music.

Think about everything you know and use it as a sort of filter for how you might come alongside her. Is this action something she would appreciate and find meaningful?

What do you know about your friend's personality? Do you know any of her personality types? Write down as many details as you know.

_____

_____

_____

_____

_____

What do you know about your friend's preferences? What does she like? What does she gravitate toward?

_____

_____

_____

_____

_____

How can you use this information to tailor your care to your friend and ensure it is meaningful to her?

_____

_____

_____

_____

_____

CHAPTER TWENTY

Closeness of Relationship

"And may the Lord make your love for one another and for all people grow and overflow, just as our love for you overflows." (1 Thessalonians 3:12)

Finally, you want to think about the closeness of your relationship with your friend. I learned from Marissa Henley, author of *Loving Your Friend Through Cancer*, about this idea of inner circle, middle circle, and outer circle friends.

The big idea is that the closer you are to a friend, the more intimate a task you can do for them. I think we all know that, but sometimes we don't consider it when it comes to discerning how we can best help someone.

I can support my sister in a way that is more personal than I might another woman from church because I know my sister, I grew up with her, and we are comfortable around each other. I might have a good friend from church, but maybe I've never been over to her house, and so any type of care that involves cleaning or helping with their dogs or taking over food would be a bit more difficult. The closeness of the relationship just isn't there.

Let's consider an example: a friend from church is in the hospital. Is she comfortable with you seeing her sick? Or would she rather receive a card or some other form of care from you? Maybe she'd love you to set up a meal train for her family since she isn't able to cook for them.

Or maybe a friend just had surgery and has to give herself shots for a while. Is your friendship close enough that she is okay with you knowing that? Is she okay with you watching? Or would she prefer some privacy?

Personal care is especially tough for people to receive, so unless you are family or incredibly close, chances are, that is best left to those with whom she is more comfortable. But that doesn't mean you can't help. Just look for things within your level of intimacy.

Anything involving personal care is super intimate. Being in her house is pretty intimate, too, along with doing laundry for her. These kinds of tasks are reserved for inner circle friends.

Middle circle friends might set up meals, help pick up kids from school, or mow the yard.

Outer circle friends are best to stick with things like sending notes or text messages or joining in any group efforts to care for a friend or family in your church who is going through a difficult situation.

Of course, these are generalizations. Let the Lord guide you in each situation and see what He nudges you to do!

How would you "rate" your level of closeness to this particular friend? Are you in her inner circle, middle circle, or outer circle?

_____

_____

_____

_____

_____

What does that information indicate to you about ways you might be able to reach out to her in this difficult season?

_____

_____

_____

_____

_____

Look up 1 Thessalonians 3:12 in your Bible and copy it in your journal. How is God speaking to you through this verse?

_____

_____

_____

_____

_____

CHAPTER TWENTY-ONE

Knowing Your Friend

"So two good things will result from this ministry of giving—the needs of the believers in Jerusalem will be met, and they will joyfully express their thanks to God." (2 Corinthians 9:12)

This section was all about knowing your friend. It's important to become a student of her, in a sense—to learn what she likes and doesn't like, to identify what is important to her, and to listen for what she needs in this season.

So, take everything you've learned about your friend in this section and start piecing it together.

Expressed Needs: What does she want (or *not* want)?

Love Language: Which love language does she resonate with the most?

Personality and Preferences: How does her personality impact the way you come alongside her?

Closeness of Relationship: What would she be comfortable with?

You can imagine it as a giant Venn diagram with overlapping circles. The place where most of these things meet is a perfect place for you to serve.

Let's look at an example.

Megan is struggling with depression. You've known her for a few years from Bible study, and as you talk with her after church one day, you notice that she is overwhelmed and tired. She's not sleeping well at all, and she's too tired to fix meals, which means she is constantly grabbing take-out.

She works from home as a graphic designer, yet she is having a hard time getting her projects done on time. Her creativity has vanished; her children, as much as she loves them, are driving her nuts; and her husband works second shift, so he is gone during the main part of the day and only home in the mornings and late evenings.

You drive home thinking and praying about how you can support her. It breaks your heart to see her so down and worn out, feeling hopeless that anything will change. You know you can't fix it for her, per se, but you *can* show up and support her and show her you care.

When you get home, you make a list of what you know from your conversation:

- Depressed
- Not sleeping
- Not eating well
- Not getting work done on time
- Needs a break from the kids

Then you start jotting down what you've learned as you've gotten to know her over the past few years:

- Extraverted
- Likes to hang out with friends
- Prefers a clean and tidy space
- Usually sends a card on birthdays and special occasions
- Doesn't like to be the center of attention

As you pray about how to help, you pick up on some overlapping themes:

- She works from home, but she likes to be around other people.
- If she's so tired, she probably hasn't been keeping up with the house like she likes to.
- You've been to her house maybe six times or so over the past year—not a lot, but enough to feel comfortable there.

Putting it all together, you realize that she might need a morning or evening off to herself so she can hang out with friends and enjoy that time with them. Maybe you could volunteer to come over one day after school to take care of the kids. When you come, you can bring some freezer meals that are healthy and easy to warm up for the next few nights, and you and the kids make a game out of tidying the house so that it's clean when she returns home.

You also decide to write her a note that she can find after she comes home that night. Something that will encourage her and inspire her to persevere, even though the days might be hard.

Since Megan doesn't like to be the center of attention, you don't mention anything to anyone else right now. Not without asking her first. You're sure others would love to help with some meals for a few weeks or set up playdates with her kids, but again, you'll wait to talk to her before sharing with others.

See how this might all play out? Of course, when you put it within the entire C.A.R.E. framework, you can also look to see which parts of this are most authentic to *you*. If watching the kids is good for you but fixing a meal is not, you can ask someone else to make the meal for you and still be discreet about who it's for.

Keep in mind, you don't have to do *everything*. God will call different people to do different things. He'll invite one friend to be an emotional support while He nudges someone else to be a practical support with the kids, and yet another to be a support in the home with meals and cleaning. It's not all up to you! It's a team effort. (Or should I say, it's a "body of Christ" effort—everyone working together.)

First Peter 4:11 says, "Do you have the gift of helping others? Do it with all the strength and energy that God supplies."

You don't have to do this alone, my friend. God *will* guide you. He'll give you that sacred nudge to do something, and He'll give you the courage and strength to do it. So lean on Him!

Become a student of your friend. What do you know about her that will help you reach out to her in this specific situation?

_____

_____

_____

_____

_____

Do you see any areas within your friend that match your characteristics, skills, and experience? Write those down.

_____

_____

_____

_____

_____

How do we balance caring authentically for our friends with serving them in a way that is meaningful for *them*?

_____

_____

_____

_____

_____

Ask God to show you how He wants you to reach out to your hurting friend, and whether you have areas that match or not. We always need to be trusting Him to lead us! Take note of what He shares with you.

_____

_____

_____

_____

_____

CONCLUSION

Don't Let Fear Stop You

efore we end, I just want to have a bit of a heart-to-heart conversation with you about something I feel so many of us get stuck in, and that is failure.

We each define failure in a very personal way. To some, this might look like not being able to pay all your bills on time, or not being able to keep a clean house, or not reaching a goal you have. You know what failure looks like for you in this season of your life.

When I was younger, I loved school and I loved to learn. (I still do! If I could be a professional student, that'd be the perfect job for me.) Because of this, I often got good grades. One day, I came home with a C on a midterm report, and I was just so frustrated and embarrassed because it wasn't an A. It wasn't even a B. It was a C! And to me, that was failing.

These days, I often feel like I fail when I can't keep the house as clean as I want it, or I don't meet my business and ministry goals. I tend to beat myself up about it. I start to doubt and question what I'm doing.

But failure isn't limited to these kinds of situations, and what I want to focus on right now is when we "mess up" when it comes to caring for those around us.

We say the wrong thing.

We do the wrong thing.

We don't send the card like we were going to.

We give a gift card to a restaurant instead of cooking a meal at home like we wanted.

We ignore the hurt and don't do anything at all.

And we let that failure, that mistake, sneak its way into our hearts and minds. We start telling ourselves things like, *I must not be meant to do this,* or *God needs to find somebody else,* or *I just can't do anything right; I should just stop trying.*

I know what it's like to beat myself up for something I've done that didn't go as planned. I know what it's like to play mind games with the enemy. I don't always recognize what's a lie, and I get sucked into believing something that then prevents me from reaching out the next time.

Have you been there?

I remember the times when a friend said just the

right thing to me when I was struggling and I think, *Why can't I be more like her? Why can't I respond to the hurt and pain of others with these powerful questions and reminders that point others back to Jesus?*

Or I come across a hurting friend, and before I take any sort of action to reach out to her, an image will pop up in my mind of someone with whom I *did not* respond well, and my words, my tone, actually hurt them. I just see their fallen face in my mind, and that breaks my heart and so, in this current circumstance, I think, *I don't want to hurt this friend, too.* I hesitate and take a step back and think, *I'll let someone else handle this one.*

Or I'll be praying for a friend who has been going through a rough season and want to reach out to her, but it has been so long since we've had any sort of conversation that it's now awkward. *What will they think? I should have talked to her before this. I can't believe I let it go that long.* But instead of checking in, I hide in the shame that it took so long for me to talk to her.

Can you relate to any of these? Has your own story popped up in your mind?

We all have a story where we feel like we've messed up when it comes to caring for those around us. We probably have *multiple* stories.

My friend, I don't want us to get stuck in this place of shame and failure, because that's where the enemy wants us to be. He wants us to live in fear and shame so that we don't take that step and love those around us.

I think about what might have happened if Paul had fallen prey to that shame and failure. I mean, he was persecuting Christians. He was hunting them down and tearing families apart, and everyone knew that this was what he was doing.

God tells a man named Ananias to go and pray for Paul so he could see again, and Ananias almost questions Him, like, "God, I know what this man has been doing. He's been arresting Your people. He has done terrible things." Paul's reputation proceeded him.

Then, Paul comes to meet Jesus and finds out that he was wrong about all of it. What would have happened if he had gotten stuck in that place of failure? How did he possibly get past that to the point that not only is he proclaiming Jesus as the Messiah, but he's also pretty open about his past and the mistakes that he made?

Paul had a boldness about him that only an encounter and relationship with Jesus could produce.

And friend, that's what we need. *Instead of attaching ourselves to our fears and failures, we need to attach ourselves to Jesus.*

Instead of beating ourselves up about it, instead of wallowing in the shame, instead of rehearsing in our mind everything we did wrong, we are going to take a different approach to it.

First, we're going to confess it. So right here, right

now, let's just acknowledge that we mess up. We all mess up. There is power in confession, my friend. When we confess, we are shining a light on the dark places of our lives and seeking to make things right again. We are refusing to hide.

Psalm 32:5 says, "Finally, I confessed all my sins to you and stopped trying to hide my guilt. I said to myself, 'I will confess my rebellion to the Lord.' And you forgave me! All my guilt is gone."

In essence, we are saying to God, "I know that what I did wasn't right."

And after we confess, we repent. Second Corinthians 7:9 tells us to have a godly sorrow, where the pain causes us to repent and change our ways. This pain we're feeling for having hurt our friend or not loving them well, we're going to acknowledge it and tell God that we want to do better.

Psalm 38:18 says, "But I confess my sins; I am deeply sorry for what I have done." *That's* where the godly sorrow comes in.

"God, I know what I did wasn't right, and I'm so sorry for responding in that way."

When we confess and repent, we receive God's forgiveness for it. I think this is where we often get stuck, because we can't let go of what we did. We keep beating ourselves up about it and continue to feel regret.

But 1 John 1:9 says, "...if we confess our sins to him, he is faithful and just to forgive us our sins and to cleanse us from all wickedness." Do you believe that? Are you willing to receive His forgiveness?

Last, I want to encourage you to adopt a posture of curiosity about it instead of judgment. I want you to ask questions like these:

- What made me say that to her?
- Why did I not send the card like I really wanted to? What got in the way of that?
- She is a good friend of mine; why haven't I talked to her for so long?
- What was behind my reaction? What was going on that day, that I responded with frustration rather than compassion?

It's only when we do that kind of prayerful reflection that we can begin to make some of those changes we need to make.

Let's say that I have a friend who is hurting, and it has been so long since I've talked with her that I feel awkward reaching out to her, even though I want to. I've been through this scenario enough times to know that I sometimes resent being the only one who is initiating the contact. I don't like that. It begins to feel very one-sided and I'm pursuing a friendship that the other person isn't interested in. And so, I stop.

But what I see and experience on my end isn't always the case. Sometimes they just don't have the energy to reach out to me first. Sometimes they are going through such a difficult time that it's hard to see past what's right in front of them. So, at times, what I perceive as not being interested in friendship isn't really true at all.

It's only when I stop and prayerfully reflect on what's going on that I can, with God's help, uncover what might be going on inside of me that prevents me from reaching out like I know He wants me to.

Friend, I want to encourage you that, even in our failures, God can use us. He can use you. We will not do this encouragement and care thing perfectly every time. We'll mess up, make mistakes, and have hard days.

But we can't let our failures stop us from caring about others. We have to put our faith and trust in the One who will never fail.

Deuteronomy 31:6 says, "So be strong and courageous! Do not be afraid and do not panic before them. For the Lord your God will personally go ahead of you. He will neither fail you nor abandon you."

Will you pray with me?

God, I know how easy it is to feel defeated and hopeless when we just can't seem to say or do the right thing for a friend who is struggling. I know how easy it is for us to hide beneath our shame and guilt instead of bringing it before You. And so, God, today we just confess those times when we've fallen short in our care for someone else. And we are so incredibly sorry for that. It bothers us so much. Would You help us to not let the failure prevent us from trying again? Give us the courage and the strength to keep reaching out to those who so desperately need a taste of Your grace and compassion. In Jesus' name we pray, amen.

JOURNAL

What is your biggest takeaway from this book?

_____

_____

_____

_____

_____

Where were you most challenged?

_____

_____

_____

_____

_____

How do you believe God is calling you to reach out to
those around you in this season of your life?

_____

_____

_____

_____

_____

Which Bible passage spoke most to you? Write it out.

_____

_____

_____

_____

_____

Which obstacle is the one you identify with the most?
How does this show up for you?

_____

_____

_____

_____

_____

How will you use your characteristics, skills, experiences, and personality to care for others?

_____

_____

_____

_____

_____

What did you discover about how God speaks to you?

_____

_____

_____

_____

_____

Did you have a specific friend in mind when you
went through this book? If so, were you able to pin-
point specific, meaningful ways to support him/her?

_____

_____

_____

_____

_____

What additional questions do you have?

_____

_____

_____

_____

_____

APPENDIX A

Write Your Story

If you've never felt comfortable sharing your story with a friend or family member before, I invite you to take some time to write it out. You can write in narrative form, telling the story as it happened, or you can jot down keywords and phrases as they come to mind. Repeat it for each experience you wrote down in section two.

Take it easy. This is not something to rush through. You can take small steps and get it written piece by piece. This is especially important if your story feels overwhelming or includes trauma.

If you would like support as you begin to explore your story, I invite you to consider joining Journal Gently. This program is designed to help you process grief and trauma together with God through writing.

It's a gentle and healthy way to approach those hard places in your life. You can learn more at lovedoesthat.org/journalgently.

Scripture Writing

Scripture writing is a powerful way to slow down and savor God's Word. It allows us to really think about what we're reading rather than quickly reading it and then forgetting about it as we go on with our day. Below, you'll find a 30-day Scripture writing plan based on Bible verses about care, courage, and compassion.

It's simple:

- Look up the verse.
- Read through it slowly.
- Handwrite it onto another sheet of paper.
- Spend time praying about what you are reading and writing.

Materials you'll need:

- Your Bible.
- Paper. It can be notebook paper, computer paper, a journal, or whatever you want to use!
- Something to write with. A pen or pencil is fine. If you want to get artistic or colorful, maybe grab some markers or colored pencils.

Day 1: Exodus 34:6
Day 2: 1 Chronicles 28:20
Day 3: Psalm 145:9
Day 4: 1 Timothy 5:3
Day 5: Isaiah 49:13
Day 6: Matthew 9:36
Day 7: Matthew 14:14
Day 8: Acts 27:25
Day 9: Luke 7:13
Day 10: Ezra 8:23
Day 11: Luke 15:20
Day 12: 1 John 3:17
Day 13: Luke 6:36
Day 14: Philippians 2:1
Day 15: Mark 1:41
Day 16: Philippians 4:19
Day 17: 1 Thessalonians 5:14
Day 18: Psalm 31:24
Day 19: Galatians 6:3
Day 20: Romans 12:13

Day 21: 1 Corinthians 16:13
Day 22: Deuteronomy 31:6
Day 23: 1 Peter 5:7
Day 24: Psalm 112:4
Day 25: Luke 10:33
Day 26: Job 11:18
Day 27: Psalm 27:14
Day 28: Isaiah 30:18
Day 29: Psalm 106:30
Day 30: Matthew 14:27

REFERENCES

- *The Art of Comforting*, by Val Walker
- *The Sacred Echo*, by Margaret Feinberg
- *Five Love Languages*, by Gary Chapman
- *Loving Your Friend Through Cancer*, by Marissa Henley

ABOUT THE AUTHOR

Seeing far too many people go through hardship alone, Kari Bartkus became determined to show up and be present when those around her were hurting. Through her work at Love Does That, she serves as a spiritual director to hurting Christian women, but she uses a modern-day letter writing approach perfect for those drawn to quiet spaces and written words. Learn more at https://lovedoesthat.org.

Made in the USA
Monee, IL
29 January 2024

52338454R00098